G000255213

ALWAYS AND FOREVER

An Hachette UK Company
www.hachette.co.uk

Summersdale Publishers Ltd
Part of Octopus Publishing Group Limited
Carmelite House
50 Victoria Embankment
LONDON
EC4Y 0DZ
UK

www.summersdale.com

Printed and bound in Croatia

ISBN: 978-1-78685-272-4

Substantial discounts on bulk quantities of Summersdale books are available to corporations, professional associations and other organisations. For details contact general enquiries: telephone: +44 (0) 1243 771107 or email: enquiries@summersdale.com.

To......................................

From..................................

THERE IS ONLY
ONE HAPPINESS
IN LIFE: TO LOVE
AND BE LOVED.

GEORGE SAND

LOVE
UNLOCKS
DOORS
AND OPENS
WINDOWS
THAT WEREN'T
EVEN THERE
BEFORE.

MIGNON McLAUGHLIN

THE HIGHEST
HAPPINESS ON
EARTH IS MARRIAGE.

WILLIAM LYON PHELPS

LOVE

CONQUERS

ALL ♥

LOVE IS THAT CONDITION
IN WHICH THE HAPPINESS
OF ANOTHER PERSON IS
ESSENTIAL TO YOUR OWN.

ROBERT A. HEINLEIN

TO GET THE
FULL VALUE OF
JOY YOU MUST
HAVE SOMEBODY TO
DIVIDE IT WITH.

MARK TWAIN

HAPPY MARRIAGES
BEGIN WHEN WE
MARRY THE
ONES WE LOVE,
AND THEY BLOSSOM
WHEN WE LOVE THE
ONES WE MARRY.

TOM MULLEN

A MARRIED COUPLE ARE WELL SUITED WHEN BOTH PARTNERS USUALLY FEEL THE NEED FOR A QUARREL AT THE SAME TIME.

JEAN ROSTAND

LOVE
LOVES TO LOVE
LOVE.

JAMES JOYCE

LOVE IS
COMPOSED OF
A SINGLE SOUL
INHABITING
TWO BODIES.

ARISTOTLE

THE MOST BEAUTIFUL THING TO SEE IS THE PERSON YOU LOVE SMILING

LET'S RIDE

THE WAVES

TOGETHER

IF WE ARE BOLD, LOVE STRIKES AWAY THE CHAINS OF FEAR FROM OUR SOULS.

MAYA ANGELOU

MARRIAGE IS
NOT JUST SPIRITUAL
COMMUNION, IT IS
ALSO REMEMBERING
TO TAKE OUT
THE TRASH.

JOYCE BROTHERS

NO MAN OR
WOMAN REALLY
KNOWS WHAT
PERFECT LOVE IS
UNTIL THEY HAVE
BEEN MARRIED
A QUARTER OF
A CENTURY.

MARK TWAIN

LOVE MUST BE
AS MUCH A LIGHT,
AS IT IS A FLAME.

HENRY DAVID THOREAU

ROMANCE IS
THE GLAMOUR WHICH
TURNS THE DUST OF
EVERYDAY LIFE INTO
A GOLDEN HAZE.

ELINOR GLYN

COME, LET'S BE
A COMFORTABLE
COUPLE AND
TAKE CARE OF
EACH OTHER!

CHARLES DICKENS

KISS ME,
AND YOU WILL
SEE HOW
IMPORTANT
I AM.

SYLVIA PLATH

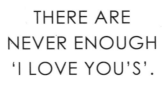

THERE ARE
NEVER ENOUGH
'I LOVE YOU'S'.

LENNY BRUCE

LOVE IS
EVERYTHING
IT'S CRACKED
UP TO BE...
IT REALLY IS
WORTH FIGHTING
FOR, BEING BRAVE
FOR, RISKING
EVERYTHING FOR.

ERICA JONG

LOVE
TURNS AN
ORDINARY
LIFE INTO A
FAIRY TALE

TOGETHER IS

A WONDERFUL

PLACE TO BE ❤

LOVE!
LOVE UNTIL
THE NIGHT
COLLAPSES.

PABLO NERUDA

BEING MARRIED IS LIKE HAVING A COLOUR TELEVISION SET. YOU NEVER WANT TO GO BACK TO BLACK AND WHITE.

DANNY PERASA

REAL LOVE
STORIES NEVER
HAVE ENDINGS.

RICHARD BACH

LOVE DOESN'T MAKE
THE WORLD GO ROUND;
LOVE IS WHAT MAKES
THE RIDE WORTHWHILE.

FRANKLIN P. JONES

GROW OLD
ALONG WITH ME!
THE BEST IS
YET TO BE.

ROBERT BROWNING

OUR
WEDDING
WAS MANY
YEARS AGO. THE
CELEBRATION
CONTINUES TO
THIS DAY.

GENE PERRET

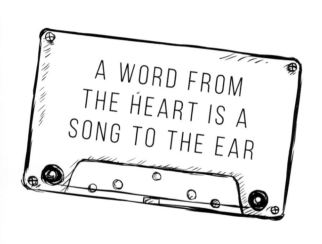

BEING DEEPLY
LOVED BY
SOMEONE GIVES
YOU STRENGTH,
WHILE LOVING
SOMEONE DEEPLY
GIVES YOU
COURAGE.

LAO TZU

TO THE WORLD
YOU MAY JUST BE
ONE PERSON, BUT TO
ONE PERSON YOU
MAY BE THE WORLD.

ANONYMOUS

MARRIAGE
SHOULD BE A
DUET — WHEN
ONE SINGS, THE
OTHER CLAPS.

JOE MURRAY

IT'S
WONDERFUL
TO BE WITH
SOMEONE
WHO WANTS
TO KNOW ALL
THE THINGS
INSIDE
YOUR HEAD

I WANT YOU

TODAY AND

EVERY DAY ♥

LOVE IS KEEPING THE PROMISE ANYWAY.

JOHN GREEN

TO FIND SOMEONE
WHO WILL LOVE YOU
FOR NO REASON,
AND TO SHOWER
THAT PERSON WITH
REASONS, THAT IS THE
ULTIMATE HAPPINESS.

ROBERT BRAULT

COMING TOGETHER
IS A BEGINNING;
KEEPING TOGETHER
IS PROGRESS;
WORKING TOGETHER
IS SUCCESS.

HENRY FORD

THE SOUND OF A KISS IS
NOT SO LOUD AS THAT OF
A CANNON, BUT ITS ECHO
LASTS A DEAL LONGER.

OLIVER WENDELL HOLMES SR

YOU HAVE
MY WHOLE
HEART FOR MY
WHOLE LIFE.

FRENCH PROVERB

I KNOW BY
EXPERIENCE
THAT THE
POETS ARE
RIGHT: LOVE
IS ETERNAL.

E. M. FORSTER

IN A SEA OF PEOPLE MY EYES
WILL ALWAYS SEARCH FOR YOU

A WEDDING ANNIVERSARY IS THE CELEBRATION OF LOVE, TRUST, PARTNERSHIP, TOLERANCE AND TENACITY. THE ORDER VARIES FOR ANY GIVEN YEAR.

PAUL SWEENEY

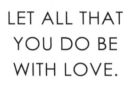

LET ALL THAT
YOU DO BE
WITH LOVE.

1 CORINTHIANS 16:14

IN DREAMS
AND IN LOVE
THERE ARE NO
IMPOSSIBILITIES.

JÁNOS ARANY

YOU WILL
FOREVER BE
MY ALWAYS

WE ARE MY

FAVOURITE

LOVE STORY ♥

FRIENDSHIP IN MARRIAGE IS THE SPARK THAT LIGHTS AN EVERLASTING FLAME.

FAWN WEAVER

IN LOVE THE
PARADOX OCCURS
THAT TWO BEINGS
BECOME ONE AND
YET REMAIN TWO.

ERICH FROMM

THE REAL ACT
OF MARRIAGE
TAKES PLACE
IN THE HEART,
NOT IN THE
BALLROOM OR
CHURCH OR
SYNAGOGUE.

BARBARA DE ANGELIS

YOU COME TO LOVE NOT BY
FINDING THE PERFECT PERSON,
BUT BY SEEING AN IMPERFECT
PERSON PERFECTLY.

SAM KEEN

TO LOVE
IS TO RECEIVE
A GLIMPSE OF
HEAVEN.

KAREN SUNDE

LOVE IS THE
STRONGEST
FORCE
THE WORLD
POSSESSES.

MAHATMA GANDHI

MARRIAGE
IS A MOSAIC
YOU BUILD WITH
YOUR SPOUSE.

JENNIFER SMITH

IF MUSIC BE
THE FOOD OF LOVE,
PLAY ON.

WILLIAM SHAKESPEARE

HE IS NOT
A LOVER WHO
DOES NOT LOVE
FOREVER.

EURIPIDES

IF I COULD
LIVE MY LIFE
AGAIN, I
WOULD FIND
YOU SOONER
SO I COULD
LOVE YOU
FOR LONGER

WE'RE

BETTER

TOGETHER

COME LIVE IN MY HEART AND PAY NO RENT.

SAMUEL LOVER

THE BEST
THING TO HOLD
ONTO IN LIFE IS
EACH OTHER.

AUDREY HEPBURN

THERE'S NO BAD
CONSEQUENCE TO
LOVING FULLY, WITH
ALL YOUR HEART.

REESE WITHERSPOON

FOR, YOU SEE, EACH
DAY I LOVE YOU MORE,
TODAY MORE THAN
YESTERDAY AND LESS
THAN TOMORROW.

ROSEMONDE GÉRARD

LOVE IS MOST
NEARLY ITSELF WHEN
THE HERE AND NOW
CEASE TO MATTER.

T. S. ELIOT

LOVE IS SOMETHING ETERNAL; THE ASPECT MAY CHANGE, BUT NOT THE ESSENCE.

VINCENT VAN GOGH

YOUR MARRIAGE
WILL NOT BE DEFINED
BY THE SIZE OF YOUR
STRUGGLES BUT
BY THE SIZE OF YOUR
COMMITMENT TO
OVERCOME THE
STRUGGLES
TOGETHER.

DAVE WILLIS

WE LOVE
BECAUSE IT
IS THE ONLY TRUE
ADVENTURE.

NIKKI GIOVANNI

TRUE LOVE
IS THE JOY
OF LIFE.

ANONYMOUS

LOVE, LAUGHTER AND HAPPILY EVER AFTER

WE MAKE

THE BEST

TEAM EVER ♥

THE SUPREME HAPPINESS OF LIFE CONSISTS IN THE CONVICTION THAT ONE IS LOVED... IN SPITE OF ONE'S SELF.

VICTOR HUGO

A JOURNEY IS
LIKE MARRIAGE.
THE CERTAIN WAY
TO BE WRONG
IS TO THINK YOU
CONTROL IT.

JOHN STEINBECK

LOVE
VANQUISHES
TIME.

MARY PARRISH

ROMANCE IS THINKING
ABOUT YOUR SIGNIFICANT
OTHER, WHEN YOU ARE
SUPPOSED TO BE THINKING
ABOUT SOMETHING ELSE.

NICHOLAS SPARKS

SUCCESS IN
MARRIAGE DOES NOT
COME MERELY THROUGH
FINDING THE RIGHT MATE,
BUT THROUGH BEING
THE RIGHT MATE.

BARNETT R. BRICKNER

ONE DOES
NOT FALL 'IN' OR
'OUT' OF LOVE.
ONE GROWS
IN LOVE.

LEO BUSCAGLIA

I LOVE HOW
WE GROW
TOGETHER

LIKE GOOD WINE,
MARRIAGE GETS
BETTER WITH AGE.

GENE PERRET

BUT TO SEE HER
WAS TO LOVE HER;
LOVE BUT HER,
AND LOVE FOREVER.

ROBERT BURNS

LOVE
GROWS MORE
TREMENDOUSLY
FULL, SWIFT,
POIGNANT,
AS THE YEARS
MULTIPLY.

ZANE GREY

LOVE IS IN THE LITTLE THINGS

THIS IS

TRUE

LOVE

THE HEART HAS ITS REASON WHICH REASON KNOWS NOT.

BLAISE PASCAL

TRUST IS A MARK
OF COURAGE AND
FIDELITY IS A MARK
OF STRENGTH.

E. M. FORSTER

FOREVER IS COMPOSED OF NOWS.

EMILY DICKINSON

TO LOVE ABUNDANTLY
IS TO LIVE ABUNDANTLY,
AND TO LOVE FOREVER
IS TO LIVE FOREVER.

HENRY DRUMMOND

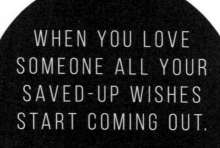

WHEN YOU LOVE
SOMEONE ALL YOUR
SAVED-UP WISHES
START COMING OUT.

ELIZABETH BOWEN

NOTHING IS TOO MUCH TROUBLE FOR LOVE.

DESMOND TUTU

LOVE ISN'T A WORD; IT'S AN ACTION

BLESSED IS THE
INFLUENCE OF
ONE TRUE, LOVING
HUMAN SOUL
ON ANOTHER.

GEORGE ELIOT

BUT WE LOVED
WITH A LOVE
THAT WAS MORE
THAN LOVE.

EDGAR ALLAN POE

I WANT
TO DO WITH
YOU WHAT
SPRING DOES
WITH THE
CHERRY TREES.

PABLO NERUDA

WE
COMPLETE
EACH OTHER

YOU'RE THE

SPRING IN

MY STEP ❤

INDEED, THE IDEAL STORY IS THAT OF TWO PEOPLE WHO GO INTO LOVE STEP FOR STEP.

ROBERT LOUIS STEVENSON

LOVE IS LIKE AN
ETERNAL FLAME –
ONCE IT IS LIT,
IT WILL CONTINUE
TO BURN FOR
ALL TIME.

KAMILA SHAMSIE

IT IS ONLY LOVE WHICH SETS US FREE.

EMILY DICKINSON

I HAVE BEEN LOVING
YOU A LITTLE MORE
EVERY MINUTE SINCE
THIS MORNING.

VICTOR HUGO

MAY YOU LIVE
AS LONG AS YOU
WISH AND LOVE AS
LONG AS YOU LIVE.

ROBERT A. HEINLEIN

HAVE A HEART
THAT NEVER
HARDENS,
AND A TEMPER
THAT NEVER TRIES,
AND A TOUCH THAT
NEVER HURTS.

CHARLES DICKENS

LOVE IS
NOT LOVE
WHICH ALTERS
WHEN IT
ALTERATION
FINDS.

WILLIAM SHAKESPEARE

A HAPPY
MARRIAGE
IS A LONG
CONVERSATION,
WHICH ALWAYS
SEEMS TOO SHORT.

ANDRÉ MAUROIS

LOVE BEARS
ALL THINGS,
BELIEVES ALL
THINGS, HOPES
ALL THINGS,
ENDURES ALL
THINGS.

1 CORINTHIANS 13:7

I AM
SMITTEN
WITH YOU

LET'S

TALK UNTIL

DAWN

TRUST YOUR HEART
IF THE SEAS CATCH
FIRE (AND LIVE
BY LOVE THOUGH
THE STARS WALK
BACKWARD).

E. E. CUMMINGS

LOVE IS NOT
CONSOLATION,
IT IS LIGHT.

SIMONE WEIL

WHO,
BEING LOVED,
IS POOR?

OSCAR WILDE

EACH MOMENT OF A
HAPPY LOVE'S HOUR IS
WORTH AN AGE OF DULL
AND COMMON LIFE.

APHRA BEHN

WHEN YOU LOOK
AT ME, WHEN YOU
THINK OF ME, I AM
IN PARADISE.

WILLIAM MAKEPEACE THACKERAY

I LOVE YOU –
I AM AT REST
WITH YOU
– I HAVE
COME HOME.

DOROTHY L. SAYERS

WE ARE SHAPED
AND FASHIONED BY
WHAT WE LOVE.

JOHANN WOLFGANG VON GOETHE

THERE IS NO
INSTINCT LIKE THAT
OF THE HEART.

LORD BYRON

I ASK YOU
TO PASS THROUGH
LIFE AT MY SIDE –
TO BE MY
SECOND SELF,
AND BEST EARTHLY
COMPANION.

CHARLOTTE BRONTË

I LOVE
EXPLORING
NEW PLACES
WITH YOU

I LOVE THE

LIFE WE

SHARE

LOVE ISN'T SOMETHING YOU FIND. LOVE IS SOMETHING THAT FINDS YOU.

LORETTA YOUNG

I LOVE YOU
NOT ONLY FOR
WHAT YOU ARE
BUT FOR WHAT I
AM WHEN I AM
WITH YOU.

ROY CROFT

MARRIAGE, ULTIMATELY, IS THE PRACTICE OF BECOMING PASSIONATE FRIENDS.

BARBARA DE ANGELIS

YOU ARE THE BUTTER
TO MY BREAD, AND THE
BREATH TO MY LIFE.

PAUL CHILD

EVER THINE,
EVER MINE,
EVER OURS.

LUDWIG VAN BEETHOVEN

A SOULMATE IS
SOMEONE WHO
APPRECIATES
YOUR LEVEL
OF WEIRD.

BILL MURRAY

THE LAST PERSON
YOU THINK OF AT
NIGHT IS WHERE
YOUR HEART IS

YOU KNOW
YOU'RE IN LOVE
WHEN YOU CAN'T
FALL ASLEEP
BECAUSE REALITY
IS FINALLY BETTER
THAN YOUR
DREAMS.

ANONYMOUS

I LOVE YOU EVER
AND EVER AND
WITHOUT RESERVE.

JOHN KEATS

A KISS IS A LOVELY
TRICK DESIGNED
BY NATURE TO
STOP SPEECH WHEN
WORDS BECOME
SUPERFLUOUS.

ANONYMOUS

LOVE IS BEING STUPID TOGETHER.

PAUL VALÉRY

HUGS

NOURISH

THE SOUL ♥

LIFE IS THE FLOWER FOR WHICH LOVE IS THE HONEY.

VICTOR HUGO

LIFE IS BEST
WHEN YOU ARE
IN LOVE.

MICHAEL MORIARTY

LET'S MAKE
OUR DREAMS
HAPPEN

WHAT COUNTS IN MAKING A
HAPPY MARRIAGE IS NOT SO
MUCH HOW COMPATIBLE YOU
ARE, BUT HOW YOU DEAL
WITH INCOMPATIBILITY.

LEO TOLSTOY

WHERE
THERE IS
LOVE THERE
IS LIFE.

MAHATMA GANDHI

MY HEART HAS
MADE ITS MIND
UP AND I'M
AFRAID IT'S YOU.

WENDY COPE

WHAT GREATER
THING IS THERE
FOR TWO HUMAN
SOULS, THAN TO
FEEL THAT THEY ARE
JOINED FOR LIFE?

GEORGE ELIOT

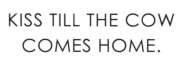

KISS TILL THE COW
COMES HOME.

BEAUMONT AND FLETCHER

IT HAS MADE
ME BETTER
LOVING YOU...
IT HAS MADE
ME WISER, AND
EASIER, AND
BRIGHTER.

HENRY JAMES

I LOVE YOU TO THE MOON AND BACK

YOU MAKE

MY WORRIES

MELT AWAY ♥

WHAT I LOVE
MOST ABOUT
MY HOME IS
WHO I SHARE
IT WITH.

ANONYMOUS

MAY THIS
MARRIAGE BE
FULL OF LAUGHTER,
OUR EVERY DAY
IN PARADISE.

RUMI

THE GOAL
IN MARRIAGE
IS NOT TO
THINK ALIKE,
BUT TO THINK
TOGETHER.

ROBERT C. DODDS

I LOVE BEING MARRIED.
IT'S SO GREAT TO FIND THAT
ONE SPECIAL PERSON THAT
YOU WANT TO ANNOY FOR
THE REST OF YOUR LIFE.

RITA RUDNER

LOVE ME WHEN
I LEAST DESERVE IT,
BECAUSE THAT'S WHEN
I REALLY NEED IT.

SWEDISH PROVERB

I AM IN YOU
AND YOU IN ME,
MUTUAL IN
LOVE DIVINE.

WILLIAM BLAKE

THE BEST FRIEND
WILL PROBABLY
ACQUIRE THE BEST
WIFE, BECAUSE A
GOOD MARRIAGE
IS FOUNDED ON
THE TALENT FOR
FRIENDSHIP.

FRIEDRICH NIETZSCHE

FAITH MAKES
ALL THINGS POSSIBLE.
LOVE MAKES ALL
THINGS EASY.

DWIGHT MOODY

I CAN'T WAIT
TO SPEND THE
REST OF OUR
LIVES TOGETHER

YOU
ARE MY
SWEETHEART

If you're interested in finding out more about our books, find us on Facebook at **Summersdale Publishers** and follow us on Twitter at **@Summersdale**.

www.summersdale.com

IMAGE CREDITS